Published by
Fiennes Print

Printed by
The DaCosta Print & Finishing Company
35/37 Queensland Road
London N7 7AH

I S B N 1 903290 00 7

Introduction

The walks in this book originate from a seeking of space, inner and outer. The privilege of living in the capital is offset by a sense of constraint and overcrowding. Many people in Muswell Hill spend hours in a crowd travelling to confined work places. This book springs from one man's seeking of space in the hours of recreation granted to a busy priest.

As the contemplative Thomas Merton wrote, 'one has to be alone, under the sky, before everything falls into place and one finds his own place in the midst of it all.'

The forty walks are listed in chapters headed according to their mileage. They last from half an hour to half a day. Some are circular walks but most exploit the public transport network for the return journey. Very full route details are provided in the text so that no more than a schematic illustration is needed to give the sense and feel of each walk. There are abundant references to sites of interest in an area stretching from Highbury Fields up to Trent Country Park and from Totteridge Common across to Pickett's Lock on the River Lee.

Forty walks from Ally Pally is a handbook to help seek space in north London, the open spaces and the green spaces that provide oxygen for London. Each walk is also provided with a short saying to encourage a seeking of 'oxygen for the spirit', the replenishment of that inner space essential for us to come fully alive as human beings.

I would like to thank the following for their assistance: my son, David, for helping with the diagrams, Ken Gay of Hornsey Historical Society and Leigh Hatts, both authors of local walk books, for checking the manuscript, Andy Brett of Alexandra Palace for providing the cover photograph, Clive Boutle and Kate Tattersall for reading the proofs and my wife, Anne, and other sons, John and James for their encouragement.

The Revd. Dr. John F. Twisleton

Alexandra Park Road, Wood Green

1 January 2000

Contents

One Mile Walks

Two Mile Walks

Three Mile Walks

Four Mile Walks

Five Mile Walks

Six Mile Walks

Seven Mile Walks

Eight to Twenty Mile Walks

Further Reading

One Mile Walks

1.1 Alexandra Palace Circular 0.8 *mile*

A short walk with a panoramic view of London. The rich history of Alexandra Palace is evoked, notably by access to the impressive Palm Court.

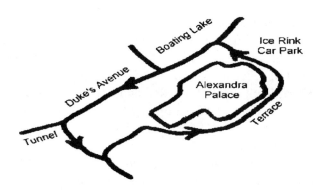

Slower together is better than faster alone. *Anon*

The Alexandra Palace was opened on Queen Victoria's birthday, 24 May 1873, after the purchase earlier, in 1863, of land from Tottenham Wood Farm to create a 240 acre park. Park and Palace took a name honouring the then Princess of Wales. Just over a fortnight later on 9 June a red-hot coal from a worker's brazier caused a calamitous fire.

On 1 May 1875 the Palace reopened. Activities included flower, fruit, dog and horse shows, a circus, zoo, racecourse and archery and cricket grounds as well as a Japanese village and a boating lake. In the First World War the buildings and grounds were used as barracks first for Belgian refugees and then for German internees who landscaped the grounds.

The Palace burned again on 9 July 1980. The Great Hall was gutted leaving a tangled heap of ironwork. Haringey Council reopened part of the Palace in 1988. The Ice Rink opened in 1990.

This walk encircles the main buildings. Turn left after leaving the Ice Rink entrance to follow the road down towards the boating lake and again keep left. Pass the children's playground with the adjacent 'dough-nut' sculpture to exit the grounds, continuing in the same direction along Duke's Avenue. On crossing The Avenue note the old railway station on the left closed in 1954 now run by CUFOS – Community Use for the Old Station.

After a few hundred yards turn back into the Alexandra Park through the entrance gate opposite Grove Avenue leading under an old railway arch. Turn left ascending towards the Palm Court entrance. The Palm Court is a conservatory containing giant palms, waterfalls and ornamental sphinxes. As the main entrance to the Palace it never fails to impress.

Continue past the Phoenix Bar to enjoy the view of London from the Terrace. The view spreads from the spire of St. James, Muswell Hill to that of St. Michael, Wood Green spanning Highgate, Crouch End and Hornsey. St. Paul's Cathedral dome is clearly visible in the far distance, as is Canary Wharf. Epping Forest beckons on the north east horizon. The remains of the Crystal Palace – its transmitter – can be observed far south on a clear day.

On returning to the Ice Rink car park the walk passes the blue plaque under the transmitter which reads: 'the world's first regular high definition television service was inaugurated here by the BBC 2 November 1936.'

1.2 Alexandra Park Circular *1.0 mile*

A walk of exploration around the Alexandra Park down the slopes and by way of the Animal Enclosure and Boating Lake.

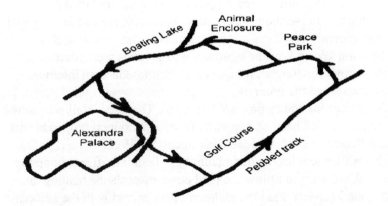

Our real journey in life is interior; it is a matter of growth, deepening, and of an ever greater surrender to the creative action of love and grace in our hearts. *Thomas Merton*

Leaving the Palace by the Ice Rink entrance, turn right past the Transmitter onto the Terrace. Take the first set of steps on the left down to the pelican. Cross the road, descend the steps and turn left. After a short distance along the path, descend the steps at the junction. Cross straight ahead and continue down the grassy slope, heading in the same direction. The towers of Holy Innocents, Hornsey and Christ Church, Crouch End and the dome of St. Joseph, Highgate come into sight. Stop at the pebbled track some distance above the cycle track, looking back to admire the Rose Window of the Great Hall and the Transmitter tower and mast.

Turn left along the pebbled track besides the Pitch and Putt Golf Course. The half-buried 'bomb' over the fence on the Golf Course is no bomb but a surviving barrage balloon anchor. The ancient tower of St. Mary's Church, Hornsey, comes into sight on the right, with Canary Wharf in the distance behind it. Turn left at the end to follow around the golf course fence up to the main road. Cross the road and continue straight ahead along the path up the grass slope, crossing the metalled path and heading towards the railings in the copse. Haringey Council's war time observation post has been renamed the Peace Park in an attempt to relinquish its military associations.

From the gate in the railings, head half right to the corner of the clearing. Go through the gap in the hedge and across a second grass clearing in the same direction. Bear right at the copse along the track through the trees. At the junction with the metalled track, before the ascent to the Palace, turn right. Follow this track around the slopes to your left, continuing straight ahead onto the tarmac road with the Animal Enclosure on your right. The local residents are used to the early morning braying of the donkeys who cohabit with the deer. There is a set of foxes and an abundance of squirrels in this part of the Park.

Continue up past the Boating Lake, open to anglers most of the year. Another early morning and late evening sound is the flight of the Canada geese who shelter on the island here. Cross to the left-hand side of the road at the lake and continue along the footpath. A fun fair is sometimes situated on the left. The walk returns besides the road up to the Ice Rink entrance through the main car park.

Two Mile Walks

2.1   **East Finchley** returning by 102 Bus   *1.6 miles*

*A stroll that captures a country atmosphere from woodland residual
from the original forest, once the haunt of highwaymen.*

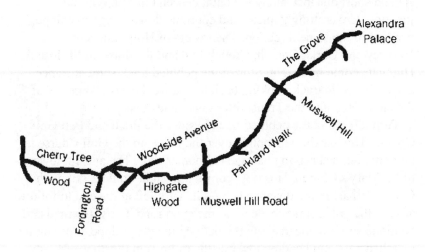

Truly it is an evil to be full of faults, but it is a still greater evil to be full of
them, and to be unwilling to recognise them. *Pascal*

Descend from the Palm Court entrance down the steps. After fifty
yards turn right past the edge of the car park into The Grove.
Continue along the tree-lined avenue on the left side, which leads
eventually over a covered footbridge. Pass down through the tunnel
under the main road to join the Parkland Walk.

There are exceptional views of London from the section below
Muswell Hill. After the Pill Box on the right pass under a road bridge
to ascend the pathway onto the pavement of Muswell Hill Road.

Turn right a few yards along the pavement through the Cranley
Gardens Gate entry to Highgate Wood. Continue from the entrance
taking the right fork following the pathway up the initial incline.
Take a right turn to leave the wood at the Bridge Gate which leads
onto Lanchester Road.

Turn right again and cross Woodside Avenue at the end of the road onto Fordington Road. Enter the cutting into Cherry Tree Woods as the road turns sharp left to continue in the same direction.

Finchley is a Saxon name meaning 'wood frequented by finches'. East Finchley is situated near to what was the northern gate of the Bishop of London's park, hence the adjacent Bishops Avenue. The notorious Finchley Common was crossed by the Great North Road and was in former days a haunt for robbers and highwaymen.

Continue through the oaks of Cherry Tree Woods to East Finchley underground station. Catch the 102 bus by the station back to Alexandra Park Road and walk up The Avenue to the Palace. This walk can be extended to Hampstead Garden Suburb (3.2), Brent Cross (6.1) or Mill Hill (8.5).

2.2 New Southgate returning by railway *1.8 miles*

The advent of the railway changed the face of this part of London in the nineteenth century. This walk exploits grassland covering a railway tunnel north of the Alexandra Palace station.

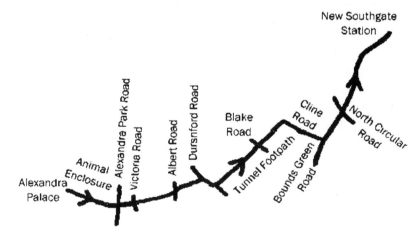

I believe in the sacredness of every human being and that each one is called to be fully alive. *Jean Vanier, founder of L'Arche communities for people with disabilities and their caregivers.*

Descend from the Ice Rink on the steep pathway, which passes the
Animal Enclosure on the left, to the open gateway onto Alexandra
Park Road. Turn right and walk down to the pedestrian crossing.
Cross and turn down Alexandra Avenue. Turn right at the end and
then immediately left down Outram Road. Turn left at the bottom
then cross to descend Albert Close. Take the cutting on the right into
Crescent Rise. Turn left and then right at the top to cross Durnsford
Road at the traffic bollards. Ascend the steps to follow the footpath
which has two sections before and after crossing Blake Road.

The pathway runs along the top of the railway tunnel. The Great
Northern Railway began in 1850. Kings Cross Station was built in
1852 when the first stations out of London were Hornsey and the
destination of this walk – New Southgate (then called Colney Hatch).

The present Alexandra Palace station was originally called Wood
Green. It was built in 1859 at a cost of £4,000 paid for by a Mr.
Rhodes. The Rhodes family owned Tottenham Wood Farm from
which the Alexandra Palace and Park were derived. The classical
portico of their farmhouse, an early nineteenth century construction,
still stands in the grounds of Rhodes Avenue School further down off
Albert Road, the extension of Durnsford Road.

Near to your crossing point from Crescent Rise is a Garden Centre
which was originally the Wood Green Lido, built in 1934.

The footpath provides striking views on looking back towards the
Alexandra Palace. After the second stretch of footpath continue on
Hillside Gardens to the end of Cline Road past a section of
Middlesex University.

Turn left at Bounds Green Road. Cross the North Circular Road
and follow Station Road to New Southgate station where trains run
regularly to Alexandra Palace station.

From the station walk up to the Palace or catch a W3 bus. This
walk can be extended to Southgate (2.7), Oak Hill Park (4.4),
Cockfosters (5.6), Coppetts Wood (7.3) or Trent Park (8.2).

2.3 **Wood Green** circular via Alexandra Palace
       Station *1.9 miles*

*Wood Green Common, the main site of historic interest on this walk,
became the nucleus of the suburb as water and rail links engaged the
community with the expanding metropolis.*

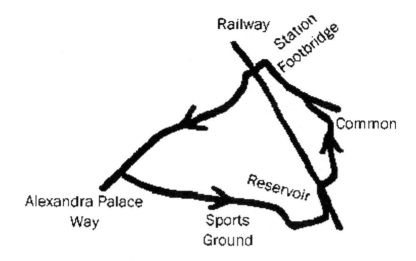

I needed to commit and focus my inner understanding and strength outside myself. *Brian Keenan, former Beirut hostage*

From the main entrance of the Great Hall descend the steps and cross Alexandra Palace Way by the pelican. Follow the path down from the road to the sports ground, passing the pavilion and heading for the bottom left hand corner of the field. This is the site of the racecourse opened in June 1868, originally the nearest course to central London. In 1970 the Jockey Club revoked the track licence and the imposing grandstand was demolished. The extensive car parks further west are built on the old paddocks.

Turn left at the playground to walk alongside the fence with the reservoir on your left. Continue along the path under the railway line. On exiting the railway tunnel turn left and follow Western Road past the Chocolate Factory Arts Centre to Wood Green Common. The present park and adjacent school were provided originally for their factory workers by the Barratt family.

Cross or skirt the Common and continue to the left and uphill along Station Road passing over the New River. It was the construction of this water conduit that provided the first connection between the growing metropolis and Wood Green, then a rural hamlet at the foot of a wooded hill. The New River was built to carry water from the Hertfordshire springs of Chadwell and Amwell along a 38 mile route which passed through Enfield, Tottenham, Hornsey and Islington to a reservoir at Sadlers Wells. Continue up to the railway station.

It was the arrival of the railway in 1859 that accelerated the creation of the now familiar Wood Green suburb. Immediately after the booking hall turn left to cross the railway on the pedestrian footbridge. Either turn left to follow the road up to the Palace or go right and left up Alexandra Park Road to enter the Palace grounds by way of the Animal Enclosure.

2.4 **Hornsey** circular via Priory Park *2.2 miles*

This walk down the slopes from Alexandra Palace to Hornsey visits the historic St. Mary's Churchyard and Priory Park, a generous portion of grassland that survived the nineteenth century expansion of London.

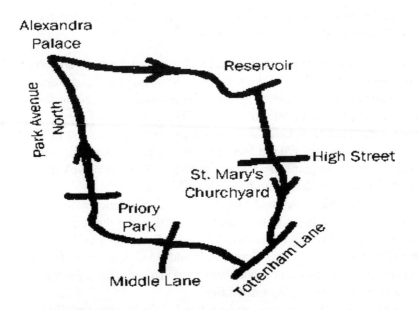

Yesterday is history, tomorrow is a mystery, today is a gift – which is why it's called the present! *Anon*

Follow Walk 2.3 to the footpath alongside the Reservoir. After fifty yards turn right down the pathway known as Cross Lane which leads to the High Street. Cross to enter St. Mary's Churchyard. Pass through the Churchyard into Glebe Road. Take the short pathway across the road at the end which leads onto Tottenham Lane just before Holy Innocents Church. Continue past the Church and turn right down Rokesley Avenue. At the junction with Middle Lane turn right and enter Priory Park.

The Priory was an early nineteenth century mansion which survived until around 1902. Priory Park was opened in 1894 on former Priory estate lands at a time when green land was threatened by the expansion of London. The granite fountain dated 1880 was moved to Hornsey from St. Paul's Cathedral Churchyard in 1909. This provides Hornsey with a link with the famous churchyard though Hornsey had the Bishop of London as Lord of the Manor from early medieval times.

Continue from the Middle Lane entrance towards a playground in the distance. Exit the park to the left of the playground and turn immediately right into an alley which leads onto Park Avenue South. Head in the same direction to cross Priory Road at the traffic bollards and ascend Park Avenue North. Pass through the playing field into the Palace grounds heading in the same northerly direction upwards to the Palace itself.

2.5 **Bounds Green** circular via Alexandra Palace Station *2.4 miles*

A circular walk around the Alexandra Palace slopes on local roads down towards Bounds Green underground station.

So many people of good will would become persons of noble soul if only they would not panic and resolve the painful tensions within their lives too prematurely. *Jacques Maritain*

Descend from the Great Hall to the left along the Terrace and then continue in the same direction across the car park. Continue down the steps and past the old fountain, following the path down the grassy slopes towards the railway station.

Notice the old bunker, now part of the Peace Park referred to in Walk 1.2. Cross the pedestrian footbridge and continue straight ahead across the zebra and around the side of The Starting Gate pub. This was built as The Palace Café in 1875. It was also known once as The Alexandra Palace Hotel. It has a fine interior with iron columns and plenty of engraved glass.

At the end of St. Michael's Terrace continue straight ahead onto
the footpath. This leads through Avenue Gardens onto Bounds Green
Road. Turn left and walk along the pavement of this busy road,
which ascends and bears left. At the top of the hill past the shops turn
left into Park Road, some distance before Bounds Green underground
station which dates from the arrival of the extended Piccadilly Line
in 1932. The underground succeeded the old electric tramways as the
major link from the new suburb to the centre of London.

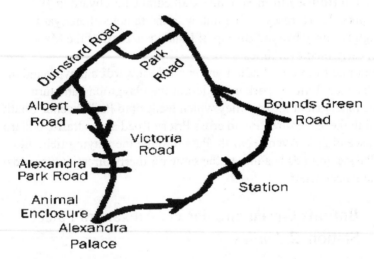

Walk down Park Road passing the College of North East London
buildings. Turn right down the pathway just after the College at the
start of Park Grove. At the top of this cutting turn left to descend
Durnsford Road over the top of the railway tunnel.

Turn left down Crescent Rise and take the alley on the right
through to Albert Close. Turn left and at the top, left again and then
right up Outram Road. Turn right at the top, then immediately left up
Alexandra Avenue to reach Alexandra Park Road. Cross at the zebra
and enter Alexandra Palace grounds by the Animal Enclosure.

2.6 **Highgate Wood** via Parkland Walk returning by
134 and 102 Buses *2.4 miles*

*The route follows a disused railway line on a path skirting Muswell
Hill, with some delightful views along a peaceful itinerary.*

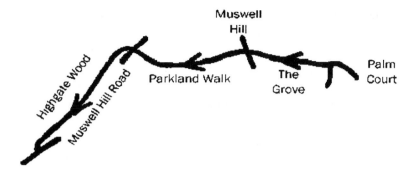

To sing the praises of God: it is that for which we were made, and it is that
which will be, for all eternity, our greatest joy.
Among Cardinal Hume's last words

Follow Walk 2.1 to Highgate Wood via The Grove and the Parkland
Walk. The Parkland Walk runs along the old railway line from
Finsbury Park to Alexandra Palace. When the railway opened in
1873 steam trains ran to the Palace from Kings Cross via Finsbury
Park and Highgate. The one-shilling (5p) fare included admission to
the Palace.

At the Cranley Gardens Gate enter the 70 acre Highgate Wood,
once the property of the Bishops of London but now run by the
Corporation of London. Turn left to follow the track parallel to
Muswell Hill Road right down to the bottom of the wood. Exit onto
Muswell Hill Road through the Gypsy Gate to catch the 134 or 43
bus back into Muswell Hill and the 102 or 299 from there to the
Maid of Muswell on Alexandra Park Road. Ascend The Avenue to
return to the Palace.

This walk may be extended to Hampstead Heath (3.7) or Finsbury
Park (4.1)

2.7 **Southgate** returning by 184 Bus *2.4 miles*

*Arnos Park preserves the valley of the Pymmes Brook and provides
one of the most beautiful walks in North London.*

I looked for my soul, but my soul I could not see. I looked for my God, but
my God eluded me. I looked for my brother and I found all three. *Anon*

Follow Walk 2.2 to the Middlesex University buildings off Bounds
Green Road. Cross the road via the traffic island, turn right and then
left down the steps to cross Tewkesbury Terrace. Follow the passage,
which crosses Maidstone Road, Shrewsbury Road and Evesham
Road and turns right into Pevensey Avenue, which is followed to the
end. Turn right, continuing up to the pelican at the major road
junction.

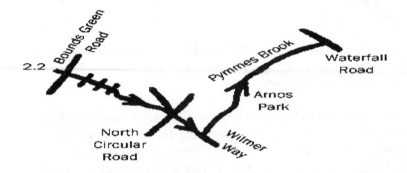

Cross the North Circular Road at the pelican, continuing straight
ahead down Wilmer Way. After the road crosses the Pymmes Brook,
turn left into Arnos Park to follow the trail alongside the brook until
the Viaduct where it reaches Waterfall Road, Southgate.

Southgate, Enfield was once a hamlet on high ground some way
from the main village of Edmonton, overlooking the Lee Valley to
the east and Barnet to the west. The name comes from being the
South Gate of Enfield Chase, enclosed around 1200. As London
expanded commercially a number of large mansions were created
here, exploiting the relative seclusion, for successful city
businessmen. Arnos Park, opened to the public in 1928, is part of the
former grounds of such a mansion. It is one of the most impressive
open spaces in north London and encloses a long stretch of the
Pymmes Brook. The brick viaduct at the end of this walk makes an
appealing feature of the necessary conveyance of the Piccadilly
underground line towards Southgate (1933).

Catch the 184 bus back from Waterfall Road to the bus stop just
beyond the junction of Alexandra Avenue and Alexandra Park Road,
adjacent to the Animal Enclosure Entrance. Alternatively, this walk
can be extended to Oak Hill Park (4.4), Cockfosters (5.6) or
Chipping Barnet (8.3).

Three Mile Walks

3.1 **Finsbury Park** via Hornsey returning by W3/rail/underground *2.6 miles*

One of several routes to Finsbury Park from the Alexandra Palace. This walk passes Churches, ancient and modern, and makes an association with David Copperfield.

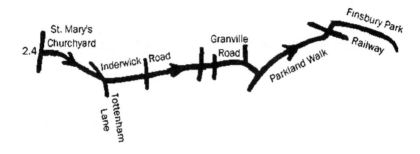

We are all in the gutter, but some of us are looking at the stars.
Oscar Wilde

Follow Walk 2.4 via the Reservoir to the ancient St. Mary's Churchyard. This Churchyard was made famous by Charles Dickens. The author made it the burial place of Betsy Trotwood's husband in *David Copperfield*. The tower of St. Mary's Church dates from around 1500. Several churches have stood on this site, the last being demolished in 1969.

Pass through the Churchyard into Glebe Road. Take the short pathway at the end which leads onto Tottenham Lane just before Holy Innocents Church. This Church, with its tall pyramid-topped tower, was clearly visible earlier in this walk from the higher slopes of Alexandra Palace. It was built by A.W.Blomfield in 1877. Blomfield also built All Saints, Highgate and the adjacent Christ Church, Crouch End.

Cross the road and descend Inderwick Road and Granville Road, passing Holy Trinity Church, Stroud Green. What used to be the Church Hall (J.S.Alder 1913) replaces the original Church (1880) which had to be demolished in 1960 following war damage.

Take a left turn just before the old railway bridge and walk the short distance along Lancaster Road to the path on the right up onto the Parkland Walk.

Turn left to follow the Walk over the pedestrian rail bridge into Finsbury Park. The cafeteria and boating lake are straight ahead. Turn right and head to the bottom of the park, then right from the gate and right again to reach the bus, underground and railway stations. The W3 bus leaves from the bus station along Stroud Green Road on the left after passing under the railway bridge.

This walk may be extended to Highbury (4.2), Stoke Newington (4.7) or the River Lee (8.4).

3.2 **Hampstead Garden Suburb** returning by 102 Bus *2.6 miles*

A stroll through the woods to East Finchley and onwards to the fascinating Hampstead Garden Suburb by the Mutton Brook.

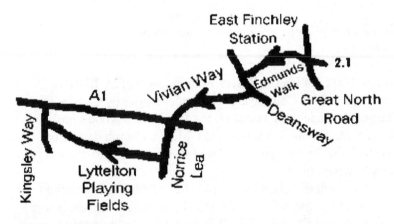

I have now come to see that thinking is a sign of imperfection. Presence, total presence of one to another, is what is ultimate, so there comes a time when having to come into the presence you have to stop thinking, otherwise you lose the awareness of the other. *Donald Nicholl approaching his death.*

Follow Walk 2.1 to East Finchley underground station. Pass through the station turning right on entering the passageway. Take a left-hand turn almost immediately to follow the passage into Edmunds Walk.

Descend from here to Deansway admiring the mock Tudor housing. Turn left and then first right down Vivian Way, following the Capital Ring footpath signs. At the very bottom cross Lyttelton Road (A1) into Norrice Lea.

The walk passes the splendid portico of Hampstead Garden Suburb United Synagogue (consecrated 1963). Take the sign-posted cutting to the right between Nos. 16 and 18 Norrice Lea. The tower of the Parish Church of St. Jude and the dome of Hampstead Garden Free Church, both by Lutyens, come into view on the horizon as the walk enters Lyttelton Playing Fields.

Continue across the field to the right hand corner exit beyond the children's playground. The path converges here with the Mutton Brook. On entering Kingsley Way turn right, ascending to the A1. Cross the road at the pelican on the left and walk the short distance to the 102 bus stop. The bus returns to the bottom of The Avenue on Alexandra Park Road. Ascend The Avenue to the Ice Rink car park at Alexandra Palace.

This walk may be extended to Brent Cross (6.1) or Mill Hill (8.5).

3.3 **Palmers Green** via Broomfield Park returning by rail *2.7 miles*

A walk to the Edwardian suburb of Palmers Green over the railway tunnel, visiting the scenic grounds of Broomfield Park.

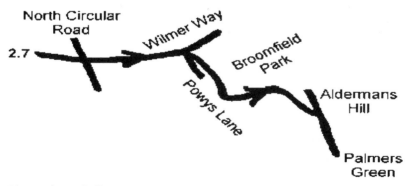

I know that I shall not die, for I am within the Life. I have the whole of Life springing up as a fountain within me. He is in my heart, he is in heaven. *Simeon the New Theologian*

Follow Walk 2.7 across Bounds Green Road and the North Circular road onto Wilmer Way. At the junction with Powys Lane enter Broomfield Park turning right along the footpath.

Palmers Green takes its origin from a hamlet adjacent to the large Broomfield estate. Broomfield House is shown on the earliest maps and was purchased from the Powys family in 1903. Now in the possession of Enfield Council, the house remains derelict, having been gutted by fires in 1984, 1993 and 1994. The municipal park remains with some of the formal garden, its ponds and lakes.

The footpath passes through a brick archway. Turn left after the bottom lake and continue keeping the lakes on your left. Turn right at the top and continue besides the football pitch on your right.

Leave Broomfield Park by the corner gate and continue on the pavement of Aldermans Hill until reaching Palmers Green station, which is on a direct line to Alexandra Palace station.

The opening of the railway in 1871 eventually changed the rural flavour of Palmers Green as a large housing development proceeded, though not until the death of a major local landowner thirty years later was building possible. The Edwardian character of the original suburb of Palmers Green is still evident.

3.4　**Queen's Wood** circular via Priory Park and Highgate Wood *2.8 miles*

This walk descends the Palace slopes towards Crouch End traversing Queen's Wood and Highgate Wood. It returns along the old railway track.

Some men see things as they are and say 'why?' I dream things that never were and say 'why not?'
Senator Edward Kennedy - Eulogy for Robert F. Kennedy

Descend from the Great Hall steps down to the main cycle track. Turn right and follow the track past the car park on your left. The track joins the main arterial exit route from the car parks down to the junction of Alexandra Palace Way, Muswell Hill, Priory Road and Park Road. Cross to Park Road. Pass across the zebra crossing at the top of Cranley Gardens and continue down Park Road.

After a short distance turn right into a fenced footpath which cuts between a number of recreation grounds. At the end of the pathway cross the road (Wood Vale) to enter Queen's Wood. The 52 acres of woodland were purchased for public use in 1886 at a cost of £30,000 and named in honour of Queen Victoria.

Continue straight ahead eventually passing the old paddling pool on your right. This is now used as a stage for dramatic presentations in the summer months. Ascend past the cafeteria on your right to Muswell Hill Road. Cross the road at the pelican and continue straight ahead into Highgate Wood.

Turn right to walk parallel to Muswell Hill Road, leaving the Wood at the Cranley Gardens Gate. Immediately descend the slope on the left to pass via the road tunnel onto the Parkland Walk. Follow the old railway line with its splendid views over north-east London, as the Alexandra Palace Transmitter comes into sight.

Pass under Muswell Hill below the bus stop and continue forward onto the covered bridge, adjacent to Muswell Hill Infants and Junior Schools. After exiting the footbridge take the right fork to walk through the tree-lined Grove.

Cross the car park to head directly via steps to the Palm Court Entrance of Alexandra Palace.

3.5   **Finchley Lido** returning by 232/134 and
102 Buses   *3.0 miles*

*This walk follows the roads to the North Circular Road and then
traverses the woodland and fields above it to Finchley.*

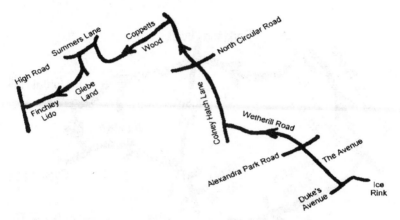

Whoever tries to dive below the calm water of his self-illusion, to humble
himself and learn his true self, experiences the even stronger thrust of his
own pride that tends to lift him above himself, so that he may emerge and
remain on the surface. *Raniero Cantalamessa on the Archimedes Principle
of the human spirit*

Follow Walk 1.1 to the park exit and turn right before Duke's Avenue
down The Avenue. Cross Alexandra Park Road by the Maid of
Muswell pub. The pub name recalls the origin of Muswell Hill.
A house in Muswell Road has a plaque marking the site of the
original well, dedicated to the Blessed Virgin Mary and claimed to
have healing properties. The Bishop of London granted land here to
the Augustinian Priory of St. Mary, Clerkenwell in the twelfth
century.
   The walk continues past the pub in roughly the same direction
along Grosvenor Road and then Wetherill Road down to Colney
Hatch Lane. Turn right and continue down to cross the North
Circular Road and a few hundred yards beyond the entrance on the
left to Coppetts Wood.
   As a more scenic alternative to the above, follow Walk 2.6 to
Muswell Hill and catch the 134 or 43 to the entrance of Coppetts
Wood on Colney Hatch Lane.

Continue into the Wood. After the steps ignore the left-hand turn. Eventually the path emerges onto a track with derelict land opposite. Turn right and continue past some cottages to Compton Sports Centre. Turn right there past the School continuing up to Summers Lane. Turn left and continue for some distance before taking another left turn into Downway. Take the footpath from there onto the Glebe Land. Continue in the same direction to exit onto the High Road just north of Finchley Lido, Great North Leisure Park.

The 232 bus stop is on the North Circular south of the Lido. Change at Colney Hatch Lane for a 134 or 43 bus to the top of Alexandra Park Road. The 102 bus runs from there to the bottom of The Avenue below the Palace. Alternatively walk up the High Road from the Lido to catch the 134 bus from its terminus at Tally Ho Corner, the junction of Woodhouse Road with the High Road at North Finchley. This walk may be extended to Totteridge (6.3) and Chipping Barnet (8.1).

3.6 **Haringey Passage** to Finsbury Park returning by W3/rail/underground *3.2 miles*

Haringey Passage provides a relatively peaceful thoroughfare for pedestrians through a busy part of North London to Finsbury Park.

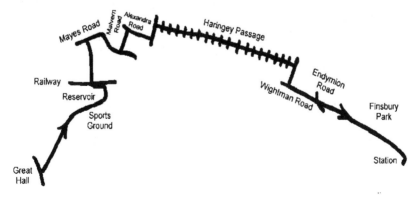

No human being is worthy to receive love. Love is a sacrament we ought only to receive on our knees with "Lord, I am not worthy" on our lips.
Oscar Wilde

Follow Walk 3.1 to the reservoir but continue along the path, which eventually enters a tunnel under the main railway line. From the railway tunnel continue straight ahead down Coburg Road onto Mayes Road. Turn right and follow the road round to cross the zebra as Mayes Road gives way to Hornsey Park Road. Continue along this road and take the first left down Malvern Road, turning right at the end along Alexandra Road and walking down to Turnpike Lane.

The Haringey Passage begins opposite Burghley Road, some fifty yards up from Alexandra Road. Continue along the Passage that cuts across fourteen parallel roads. These streets are called 'The Ladder' on this account. At Umfreville Road turn right up to Wightman Road. Turn left to cross the railway bridge and continue in the same direction along Endymion Road and the entrance to Finsbury Park.

Finsbury Park is at the junction of the boroughs of Haringey, Islington and Hackney. It was originally Hornsey Park. There is record of a visit there from the boy King Edward V during his brief reign in 1483. Edward was accompanied by his uncle and 'protector' who within weeks removed him to the Tower with his younger brother and reigned as King Richard III. Skeletons, allegedly theirs, were found there in 1674 and later buried in Westminster Abbey.

The present Finsbury Park was opened in 1869. It has a perimeter walk, a central boating lake, 'American Gardens' with rhododendrons and a cafeteria. The New River water conduit flows through a corner of the park.

Turn right at the entrance and continue to the boating lake and cafeteria. Continue further in the same southerly direction to reach the bus, underground and railway stations whose locations are described at the end of Walk 3.1. This walk may be extended to Highbury (4.2), Stoke Newington (4.7) or the River Lee (8.4).

3.7 **Hampstead Heath** returning by railway
3.5 miles

Hampstead Heath gives a picture of North London as it was centuries ago. This walk to the Heath traverses the historic Highgate Wood as well as Waterlow Park on the outskirts of Highgate Village.

My enemy is my most valued teacher. *The Dalai Lama*

Follow Walk 2.6 to the bus stop on Muswell Hill Road but continue
up to Archway Road. Turn left to walk past the Highgate
underground station entrance. At the top of Shepherd's Hill cross
Archway to descend Highgate Avenue.

At the bottom of the Avenue, take the cutting (Peacock Walk) into
Cholmeley Crescent. Turn left and then right at the roundabout to
ascend Cholmeley Park. At the top turn right and cross Highgate
High Street at the pelican.

Enter Waterlow Park keeping to the path on the right hand side,
which leads into Swains Lane. The park is named after its donor, the
philanthropist Sir Sidney Waterlow, Lord Mayor of London 1872–3,
whose statue can be seen in the grounds. Turn left at Swains Lane
and go down the hill, taking a right hand turn into Langbourne
Avenue. At the gated exit to the Avenue, cross Highgate West Hill to
enter Millfield Lane.

Take the first entry path into Hampstead Heath, passing between
the ponds and turning left at the far end. The 800 acres of heathland
provide recreational space for up to 100,000 visitors a day in the
summer. This contrasts with a quieter history as a former haunt for
wolves. In the fifteenth century the Heath was an out of the way
place where the clothes of gentry were taken to be washed. Claims of
medicinal benefit from the springs enhanced the reputation of
Hampstead. Keats, Shelley and Dickens are among the many poets
and writers who have found inspiration here.

Continue to the information office and toilets. Turn right at the
cafeteria and then left to pass the Lido on your right and exit the
Heath at Gordon House Road. Turn right and walk the short distance
to Gospel Oak station. Take the old North London Line, changing at
Highbury & Islington to return to Alexandra Palace station.

Four Mile Walks

4.1 **Parkland Walk** to Finsbury Park returning by W3/rail/underground *3.5 miles*

The closure of the railway line through Highgate provided walkers with a thin green belt across north London, familiar to all as 'The Parkland Walk'.

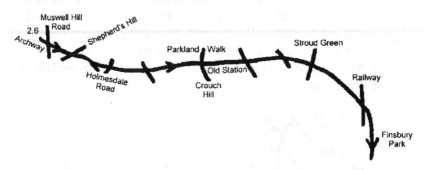

The world is full of sorrow. The root of sorrow is attachment desire.
The uprooting of sorrow is the dropping of attachment.
Anthony De Mello's three-line receipe for happiness

From the Palace follow Walk 2.6 through The Grove and Highgate Wood up onto Archway Road.

This busy road, last stretch of the A1 from the north of England, dates back to 1813 in its current form. The failure of the original attempt to tunnel through Highgate Hill and save the steep ascent was redeemed by the compromise of a cutting, since lowered. A viaduct was created (hence Archway Road) to avoid disrupting the ancient route of Hornsey Lane.

Turn left to follow the road down, crossing the top of Shepherd's Hill and turning left down Holmesdale Road after the pub. A floor mosaic at the entrance to The Shepherds pub reveal its previous name, 'The Birkbeck'. Enter the Parkland Walk on the left heading to the right, away from Highgate tunnel. The old railway track includes the ghost of Crouch End Station, built in 1870. A figure of Pan is perched high in one of the old railway arches near to a children's play area. Notice the covered reservoir on the left before Stroud Green.

The Parkland Walk crosses two active railway lines before entering Finsbury Park.

Follow the directions to rail, underground and bus stations for Alexandra Palace as described at the end of Walk 3.1. Alternatively extend this walk to Highbury (4.2), Stoke Newington (4.7) or the River Lee (8.4).

4.2 **Highbury** returning by rail/underground
4.0 miles

The walk extends a route through Finsbury Park to skirt the Arsenal Stadium, visiting Gillespie Park Nature Reserve and the historic Highbury Fields.

No-one frees anyone. No one achieves freedom alone. Human beings achieve freedom in communion. *Paolo Freire*

Take one of Walks 3.1, 3.6 or 4.1 to Finsbury Park. From the booking hall at the station cross Station Place and turn right to cross Seven Sisters Road at the pelican. The 'Seven Sisters' title is said to derive from a group of elms at the other end of this road. Walk around the Bank to descend St. Thomas's Road opposite the Mosque. Follow the marked cycle route signs heading for the Arsenal stadium.

Turn right before St. Thomas's Church down Quill Street to enter Gillespie Park Local Nature Reserve. An extension of the Parkland Walk is planned, making a more direct route from Finsbury Park to this Reserve.

Follow the track past the caféteria and turn right to enter Drayton Park. Continue down this road to the roundabout and about the same distance beyond it turn left down Whistler Street. Take the alley between 78 and 79 Whistler Street, cutting through to Framfield Road. At the other end of Framfield Road continue right along Highbury Terrace to Highbury Fields. Take the path after the first

field down onto Church Walk, turning right along this pathway
before the caféteria.

The walk enters Highbury Place, joining the footpath alongside
the Highbury Fields. Continue down to the War Memorial, adorned
with two cannons. The inscription reads: *To the Ninety-Eight
Islingtonians who died for their country in the South African War
1895–1903*. Highbury Fields playground and swimming pool are a
short distance to the right. Cross the road at the bank to Highbury &
Islington station.

Catch the railway to Alexandra Palace station or underground to
Wood Green. The W3 or 184 Bus routes run by the entrances of
Alexandra Palace or Park.

4.3   **Winchmore Hill** returning by railway *4.2 miles*

*A walk to Winchmore Hill, once a secluded community favoured by
Quakers, through the lakes and woodland of Broomfield and
Grovelands Parks.*

Trust the past to the mercy of God, the present to his love, the future to his
providence. *St. Augustine*

Follow Walk 3.3 to Broomfield Park. Turn left on reaching the
bottom lake and continue, keeping the lakes on your right. At the top
continue ahead to the small gate onto Aldermans Hill. Turn left there
and after a short distance cross the road to ascend Ulleswater Road.
At the top junction with Conway Road turn right and then left at the
end onto Fox Hill. At the junction with Bourne Hill, below The
Woodman pub cross to enter Grovelands Park.

Continue around the putting course heading left down to the lake.
Pass the bottom of the lake and turn right along the path by the

lakeside. At the end of the lake continue in the same direction, parallel with the stream in the woods. At Grovelands Bowling Club turn right through the wood, leaving the park into Seaforth Gardens.

Turn left into the Broad Walk and continue towards Winchmore Hill. Note the early eighteenth century Rowantree House among other old houses on the right just below the old village green. Continue across the bottom of The Green to Station Road and Winchmore Hill railway station, where trains run back to Alexandra Palace station.

Winchmore Hill was originally a heavily wooded area. There are tales of witches' covens. The local industry was the burning of charcoal. As a somewhat secluded area in the late seventeenth and early eighteenth centuries it became a haven for the dissenting Quakers. The Friends Meeting House dates back to 1790. Winchmore Hill developed into its present form through the eighteenth and nineteenth centuries as the woods were mostly cleared. The railway arrived in 1871.

4.4 Oak Hill Park returning by 184 bus *4.2 miles*

This walk crosses the North Circular to join the Pymmes Brook Trail through scenic Arnos Park and the Waterfall Walk to Oak Hill Park.

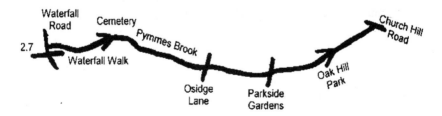

Look now forwards, and let the backwards be. *The Cloud of Unknowing*

Take Walk 2.7 to Waterfall Road and continue along the Waterfall Walk, which follows the brook below New Southgate Cemetery across Brunswick Park to Osidge Lane. Turn left to cross the lane, following the Pymmes Brook along East or West Walk. Cross Parkside Gardens into Oak Hill Park. Follow the metalled path past the pavilion, which incorporates public toilets. Continue straight ahead when this path crosses over another footpath at right angles.

The 184 bus stop for Alexandra Park Road is directly ahead on the
Oak Hill Park side of Church Hill Road. Alternatively the walk can
be extended to Cockfosters (5.6) or Trent Park (8.2).

4.5   **Great Cambridge Junction** via Pymmes Brook
returning by 102 Bus *4.2 miles*

The Pymmes Brook Trail is joined as an extension of the walk to
Palmers Green. The stream weaves along the North Circular Road
and underneath the Cambridge Roundabout.

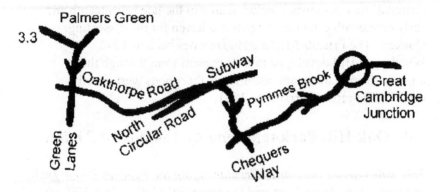

For it is not knowing a great deal that satiates and satisfies the soul but
feeling and savouring things intimately. *Ignatius Loyola*

Follow Walk 3.3 to Palmers Green station. Continue along the
pavement opposite the station as it turns south down Green Lanes.
At the pelican before the traffic lights, cross Green Lanes to head
down Oakthorpe Road. Continue, crossing the bridge over New
River, to the petrol station and follow alongside the North Circular
Road in the same direction. After a few hundred yards descend the
subway and ascend to Ostliffe Road turning left onto Chequers Way.
Turn left along Tile Kiln Lane, continuing with the Pymmes Brook
on the left, passing Oakthorpe Primary School. After passing the
Scout Headquarters continue along the footpath which runs near the
stream right along to the Great Cambridge Junction. Descend the
pedestrian underpass.
Ascend following the Pymmes Brook trail sign along the pavement

to your right. Cross the road at the pelican and cross again to the 102
bus stop for Alexandra Palace.

This walk can be extended to Edmonton Green (5.3)

4.6 Coldfall Wood circular via Bounds Green and Muswell Hill *4.2 miles*

*A pleasant circuit of Muswell Hill exploring Coldfall Wood and
Highgate Wood, returning along the old railway line.*

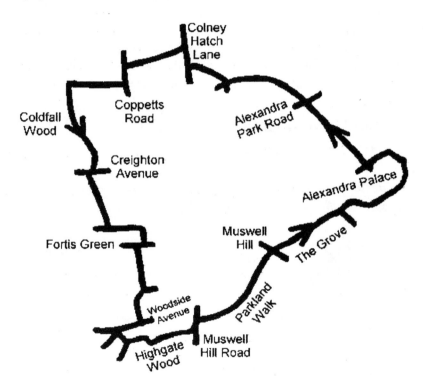

One does not see well except with one's heart; what is essential is invisible
to the eyes. *Saint-Exupery*

Follow Walk 3.5 to Colney Hatch Lane. Turn right and continue
down to St. Peter-le-Poer Church. Turn left into Albion Avenue and

cross the recreation ground onto Coppetts Road.

Turn left then right into Marriott Road. At the end of the road follow the path into the sports ground. Turn left and follow the track through Coldfall Wood onto Creighton Avenue. Turn right then left into Ringwood Avenue. At the top of the Avenue turn left to follow round Twyford Avenue to Fortis Green. Cross the road here, turning right then left down Collingwood Avenue to Tetherdown Primary School.

Follow the path that cuts down to Woodside Avenue passing the Thames Water Fortis Green Pumping Station. Cross Woodside Avenue and turn right then left into Lanchester Road. After a short distance turn left into the pathway giving access to Highgate Wood. Continue straight ahead to the Cranley Gardens Gate.

Return to Alexandra Palace along the Parkland Walk below Muswell Hill and into The Grove, as in the ending of Walk 3.4.

4.7   **Stoke Newington** returning by 67 and W3 Buses or by rail and underground   *4.5 miles*

The ancient parish of Stoke Newington, with its famous cemetery, can be explored on this walk via FinsburyPark.

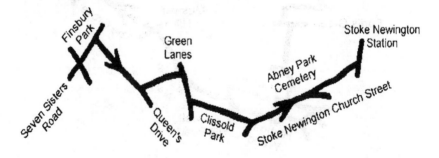

I would like to be remembered as someone who did very little harm. Most people do a great deal of harm. *Paul Eddington of 'Yes Minister' fame*

Take one of Walks 3.1, 3.6 or 4.1 to Finsbury Park. Cross the Park to take the south exit onto Seven Sisters Road. Turn left, then right, descending Queen's Drive past St. John's Church. Turn left down

Digby Crescent and left again at the junction with Brownswood
Road. Take the right turn at the traffic lights, continuing a short
distance down Green Lanes. Cross at the zebra to enter Clissold Park.
Continue straight ahead from the entrance on the path bisecting the
park with the lake on your left. Bear right at the toilets and cafeteria,
heading for the tower of St. Mary, Stoke Newington. Exit the park
opposite the Church, turning left along Stoke Newington Church
Street. Immediately on the left is the 'Ancient Mother Church of
Stoke Newington', allegedly the gift of King Athelstan around 940
AD. The Church was bombed 1000 years later in 1940. Its restoration
dates from 1953.

Continue past the shops and turn left into Abney Park Cemetery.
Stoke Newington was a former refuge for Dissenters who were
forbidden to live in the City of London. Daniel Defoe is a former
resident. In the eighteenth century many nonconformist chapels and
meeting houses were built in this locality. In the Cemetery the graves
of William and Catherine Booth greet you: *William Booth, founder
and first General of the Salvation Army. Born 1829. Born again of
the Spirit 1845. Founded the Salvation Army 1865. Went to heaven
20th August 1912.*

Turn right at this grave and continue around on the pathway to the
Information Centre. Abney Park Cemetery has several other
interesting graves including those of Dr. Watts, the hymnwriter, and
Chartist leader, James Bronterre O' Brien.

Exit onto Stoke Newington High Street, turning left to walk the
short distance to Stoke Newington railway station. Return to Wood
Green by 67 Bus, or catch a train to Seven Sisters and proceed by
underground to Wood Green station. Catch the W3 to Alexandra
Palace. This walk can be extended to the River Lee (8.4).

Five Mile Walks

5.1 **Coldfall Wood** circular via Queen's Wood and Highgate Wood *4.7 miles*

A circuit of Muswell Hill passing through all three local woods.

To be holy is to be natural.. God created nature and God's presence expresses itself through the rhythms of nature. To be in rhythm with one's nature is to be in rhythm with God. *John O'Donohue*

Follow Walk 3.4 down to Park Road and through Queen's Wood to Highgate Wood. Continue back to Alexandra Palace following the reverse of Walk 4.6, which skirts Muswell Hill to pass through Coldfall Wood, returning via Colney Hatch Lane.

5.2 **Cricklewood** via Spaniards Inn returning by railway or 245 and 102 Bus *4.8 miles*

Spaniards Inn is the midpoint and a possible source of refreshment on this walk to Cricklewood via Highgate, Kenwood Estate, the historic Old Bull and Bush pub and Childs Hill.

The question which divides men today is whether Society will be merely an immense exploitation for the benefit of the strongest or a consecration of everyone for the service of all. *Frederick Ozanam, founder of the Society of St. Vincent de Paul*

Follow Walk 2.1 into Highgate Wood at the Cranley Gardens Gate. Ignoring the main paths, head straight up the track into the wood. After a short distance, the track descends to the drinking fountain. Continue straight ahead towards the cafeteria. Follow the path, keeping the recreation ground on the right. After the children's playground and public toilets, follow the path out of the wood onto Archway Road.

   Cross at the pelican and enter Church Road across from the wood. Continue across North Hill into View Road. At the end of the road,

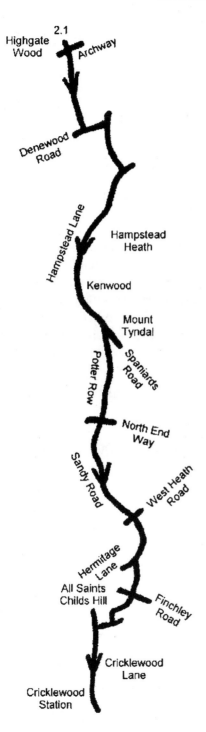

2.1
Highgate Wood
Archway
Denewood Road
Hampstead Lane
Hampstead Heath
Kenwood
Mount Tyndal
Potter Row
Spaniards Road
North End Way
Sandy Road
West Heath Road
Hermitage Lane
All Saints Childs Hill
Finchley Road
Cricklewood Lane
Cricklewood Station

turn left into Denewood Road. At the junction with Broadlands Road turn right and continue in the same direction along Bishopswood. Turn right at the end into Hampstead Lane.

Continue along Hampstead Lane passing Kenwood West and East Lodges. There is a restaurant at Kenwood House and free entrance to view the Adam Library. Continue on the left-hand pavement past the roundabout up to Spaniards Inn.

This sixteenth century Inn is said to take its name from a Spanish Ambassador to King James II. Dick Turpin stabled his horse, *Black Bess*, in the adjacent Toll House. Shelley, Keats and Byron used to drink here and Charles Dickens makes mention of Spaniards Inn in his book *Pickwick Papers*.

Continue between the Inn and Toll House, passing a cattle trough opposite Mount Tyndal. Turn right to descend Rotten Row, passing the pond on your left, descending into North End and then up to the main road.

The Old Bull and Bush pub on the road was immortalised by the Edwardian song 'Come, come, come and make eyes at me, down at the Old Bull and Bush'. The song in turn was made famous by the music–hall star Florrie Forde (1876–1940).

The pub itself dates back to the reign of Charles I starting life as a
farmhouse on the bare heath.

   Cross North End Road to enter Sandy Road. Descend with the park
railings on the right, passing between Leg of Mutton pond and the
entrance to Golders Hill Park down to West Heath Road. Cross into
Platts Lane entering Camden Borough at the cattle trough.

   Continue in the same direction along Hermitage Lane. Turn left
along Pattison Road to reach Finchley Road. Cross the main road and
enter Church Walk, descending past All Saints, Child's Hill. Turn
right out of Church Walk onto Lyndale Avenue. At the main road,
turn left and follow Cricklewood Lane across Hendon Way to reach
the station.

   Cricklewood station was opened in 1870 by Midland Railway with
massive sidings to the north. Some of the nineteenth century terraced
housing built for railway employees still survives nearby. The station
is on the Thameslink from Kings Cross where trains run to Alexandra
Palace. The 245 and 260 bus routes on Cricklewood Lane travel to
Golders Green bus station, from where the 102 bus runs to Alexandra
Park Road.

5.3 **Edmonton Green** via Wood Green returning by
102 Bus *4.9 miles*

*This walk passes through Chitts Hill and joins the Pymmes Brook
Trail on its way to Edmonton.*

The serene beauty of a holy life is the most powerful influence in the world.
Pascal

Follow Walk 2.5 to Bounds Green Road. Cross from Braemar
Avenue Baptist Church, noting the granite obelisk on the right.
This memorial to Catherine Smithies (1794–1877), temperance
campaigner and founder of the Band of Mercy Movement, is sited
incongruously before the Prince of Wales public house.

   Enter the footpath between the houses to the left of the pub, which
runs to Nightingale Road. Cross the road, noting the cattle trough on
the right, and pass through the small park and children's playground
to Truro Road. Turn right and continue across the top of Finsbury
Road to the High Road. Take another right turn and cross the pelican

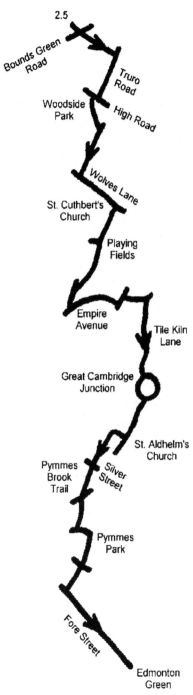

2.5
Bounds Green Road
Truro Road
Woodside Park
High Road
Wolves Lane
St. Cuthbert's Church
Playing Fields
Empire Avenue
Tile Kiln Lane
Great Cambridge Junction
St. Aldhelm's Church
Pymmes Brook Trail
Silver Street
Pymmes Park
Fore Street
Edmonton Green

to the entrance of Woodside House and Park.

Woodside House, formerly Earlham Grove Lodge, was built 1864–6 in the Italianate style. It served once as Wood Green Town Hall and included a police court. The House is now used by Haringey Social Services. The House and Park once formed part of the Chitts Hill House estate. The small Roundhouse in the corner of the Park on the High Road dating from 1821–2 was the entrance to a carriage drive to Chitts Hill House. This house, nicknamed 'the mushroom house', is one of the oldest buildings remaining in Wood Green.

Take an immediate left after the entrance gateposts and follow the diagonal path across Woodside Park. On entering Glendale Avenue note St. Thomas More School on your right with its copper domes and Baroque styling. Turn left then right along Woodside Road.

Continue down to the perimeter fence of the New River sports ground on Wolves Lane.

Turn left along the lane passing St. Cuthbert's Church, Chitts Hill, built by the architect J.S.Alder in 1906–7.

Take the first right turn down Norfolk Avenue and enter the playing fields, heading right towards the children's playground. The exit gate lies beyond this and

leads through Devonshire Court onto Devonshire Hill Lane. Turn
left, continuing along to the pathway between Nos. 106 and 108.
Take this pathway down to Empire Avenue and turn left. At the
junction with Pasteur Gardens turn left again and then right into
Chequers Way.

The Walk joins the Pymmes Brook Trail as it turns right along Tile
Kiln Lane. Continue with the brook on your left, passing Oakthorpe
Primary School on your right down to the Scout Headquarters.
Follow the footpath along the brook to the Great Cambridge Junction
roundabout. Descend the pedestrian underpass.

Ascend following the Pymmes Brook Trail signs, passing the shops
and then Aylward School on the left, opposite the toilets. Millfield
Theatre and Weir Hall Library are on the right.

Opposite St. Aldhelm's Church cross Silver Street into the grounds
of Millfield House. Cross the metal bridge and follow the brook trail.
Enter Stathan Grove passing the Free Church on your right. Cross
into Tanners End Lane and follow the Pymmes Brook pathway up to
Silver Street. Cross and enter Pymmes Park, heading past the tennis
court on your left to cross the lake by the footbridge. Turn right and
walk straight ahead with the playground railings immediately on
your right.

Exit Pymmes Park by the public toilets. Head down Park Road to
turn left at The Golden Fleece pub into Fore Street and continue
towards Edmonton Green. Catch the 102 bus back to Alexandra Park
Road from Edmonton Green Bus Station.

5.4   **Stroud Green** circular via Hornsey and Highgate Wood   *5.0 miles*

A walk down the slopes of the Palace to Hornsey and then up to
Stroud Green, returning along the Parkland Walk and passing
through Highgate Wood.

The truth cannot impose itself except by virtue of its own truth, as it makes
its entrance into the mind at once quietly and with power.
Second Vatican Council

Follow Walk 3.1 to Stroud Green and join the Parkland Walk. This
area was originally marshland before the advent of suburban housing.

Turn right and follow the Parkland Walk to Highgate. The walk
ascends to the left before the railway tunnel up to Holmesdale Road
and then onto Archway Road.

Walk down to Muswell Hill Road. Turn right then left into
Highgate Wood. Follow the path parallel to Muswell Hill Road to
exit the Wood at the Cranley Garden Gate. Descend the slope on the
left to pass via the road tunnel into the Parkland Walk. Follow the
end of Walk 3.4 along the Parkland Walk and The Grove to
Alexandra Palace.

5.5   Golders Green returning by 102 Bus *5.1 miles*

*The extensions of Hampstead Heath facilitate a country-type walk
across North London to the suburb of Golders Green.*

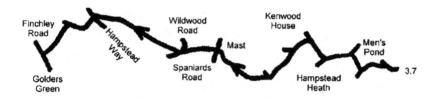

The only real test of spiritual growth is an increase of simplicity, compassion
and love. *Paul Harris*

Follow Walk 3.7 to the first Millfield Lane entrance to Hampstead
Heath, opposite No. 24, Kenwood Cottage. On entering take a sharp
right turn and walk along the hedged path besides Highgate Men's
Pond. Turn left at the end and walk between the two ponds. At the
end turn right to walk alongside the water.

At the railings before the Bird Sanctuary pond turn left and ascend
parallel to the railings. Bear right at the end of this pond between the
large trees and up the sloping meadow towards the entrance gate to
the Kenwood Estate

Kenwood House, some distance up the hill, is of neoclassical
design, remodelled 1764–79 by Robert Adam. The library is one of
his most famous interiors. Entry to both house and grounds is free.

Turn left just before the entrance gate. This walk traces the bounds
of the Kenwood Estate to Mount Tyndal. Continue along the track to

the left of the railings, passing a brick covered shelter on the right.
A little further on the track ascends and bears right by some large oak
trees past another entrance to Kenwood. Continue outside the railings
ascending through the trees. Bear left as a right fork appears towards
another entrance gate. Shortly after this junction turn right to head
again towards the black boundary railings continuing upwards
through the trees. A field appears on the left from which a transmitter
comes into sight.

Continue up to a metalled path and turn right to obtain a close view
of the mast. Follow the path left from here, alongside the old
outhouse to the left of a wooden fence. The path leads up to
Spaniards Road besides The Elms mansion.

Turn right and continue to the zebra besides Mount Tyndal. Cross
Spaniards Road here and walk straight ahead, across the top of
Rotten Row, proceeding on the pathway to the left of the railing.
This path descends to Wildwood Road. Turn left there and after
about seventy yards cross the road. Descend over the bridleway
circuit and across the field along the narrow footpath towards the
small fountain. The Church of St. Jude, Hampstead Garden Suburb,
comes into view as the walk proceeds straight ahead. After the toilets
head left diagonally across the field and then take the left fork in the
footpath onto Hampstead Way.

Cross directly into Corringham Road and continue, turning left
eventually down Rotherwick Road. Follow this road to the 102 bus
stop on Finchley Road. Take the 102 bus to the junction of Alexandra
Park Road and The Avenue leading up to Alexandra Palace.

The name 'Golders' derives from the local family known as
'Godyere', a name seen in records from the seventeenth century. The
development of the suburb of Golders Green stems from the creation
from 1903 of a tunnel under Hampstead Heath for the Northern
underground line. Two tunnels were constructed towards one another
and when they met their divergence was no more than three-quarters
of an inch. Lloyd George opened the underground in 1907.

In those days land was cheap, so that the Crematorium site was
purchased for as little as £6000 in 1902. Sir Giles Gilbert Scott was
the architect for St. Alban's Church (1932). The former music hall
known as the Hippodrome (1914) is now used by the BBC. Another
musical link with Golders Green is the ballerina Anna Pavlova who
lived at Ivy House, North End from 1912 until her death in 1931.

5.6 **Cockfosters** returning by underground and W3/184 Bus *5.1 miles*

The northern limb of the Pymmes Brook gives direction to this walk, which also follows the Piccadilly underground line to its terminus at Cockfosters.

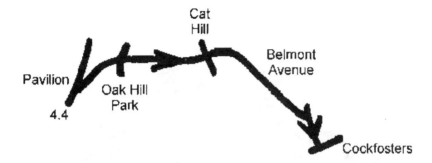

We must live life less as an attempt to conquer new land and hold on to it, and more as a grateful response to the gifts of God. *Henri Nouwen*

Follow Walk 4.4 to Oak Hill Park. At the Pavilion head north across the football pitch and after that diagonally upwards to reach the bottom of Ridgeway Avenue. Ascend the avenue and cross Cat Hill into Belmont Avenue which joins Mount Pleasant just before its junction with Cockfosters Road. Continue to this junction and cross the road to approach Cockfosters underground station.

To return take the Piccadilly line to Wood Green where the W3 and 184 Buses run to the Palace or Animal Enclosure entrance on Alexandra Park Road respectively.

Six Mile Walks

6.1   **Brent Cross** returning by 102 Bus *5.5 miles*

*Brent Cross Shopping Centre has a prime situation on the North
Circular Road. This walk to Brent Cross along the Mutton and Dollis
Brooks and their meadows provides a refreshing perspective on the
urban scene.*

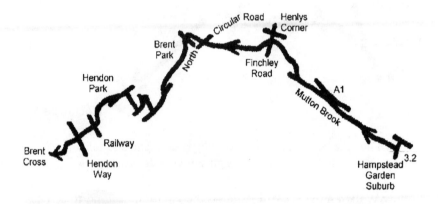

Life? I have a small notion of life from living in the body, and I feel a
moment must come when life must burst, or dance in triumph; and that is
what I expect from eternal life. *Anthony Bloom*

Follow Walk 3.2 through Lyttelton Playing Fields to Kingsley Way.
Turn right then left at the Way taking the second entry into Northway
Gardens. Continue along the path, which keeps the walled Mutton
Brook to its left, enjoying the ornamental gardens. Cross Northway
and walk onwards between the brook and the tennis courts of
Northway Park.
   At the small weir beyond the tennis courts the roar of water rivals
that of the A1 above. As the path reaches the main road turn left to
enter Addison Way. After some distance take the cutting on the right
before No. 129 to rejoin the Mutton Brook. Keep following the path
as it bends to the right on a brief return towards Addison Way. Cross
the stream after a copse and ascend to the North Circular junction
with Finchley Road at Henlys Corner.

Cross Finchley Road and descend the sign-posted route opposite, Dollis Valley Green Walk. The walk passes through the meadow immediately below the North Circular Road. It crosses eventually under the North Circular alongside the culverted brook. After a short distance turn left over the bridge at the junction of the Mutton and Dollis Brooks, continuing up Brookside Walk to the road.

Turn left then right before Lakeside Lodge to enter Brent Park. Continue past the lake, then down alongside the stream and finally up to leave the park for the North Circular again. Turn right and walk along the pavement. At the traffic lights turn right again down Brent Street. Pause a few yards down the road to admire the pool mirroring the greenery of the wood above the artificial weir.

Take the first left turn into Shirehall Park and bear left. Turn right up Shirehall Close then left at the top onto Shirehall Lane. On looking back from here the horizon is clothed in the woods of Hampstead Heath.

After a short distance enter Hendon Park and walk parallel to the road. At the bottom of the park exit and continue in the same direction under the railway bridge. Follow the pavement as it bears right at the grass roundabout. Cross Renters Avenue and follow the footpath to the left of the petrol station to enter the pedestrian underpass labelled 'Brent Cross Shopping Centre'.

At the other end of the underpass cross the road, head to the left and continue under the covered walkway. Turn left at the shopping precinct buildings, opened in 1976 on a virgin site of 52 acres, and descend the steps at the end. Turn right and continue the short distance to the bus station.

The 102 bus travels to the bottom of The Avenue, Alexandra Park Road. Ascend The Avenue to Alexandra Palace from there. The 232 bus from Brent Cross travels to Wood Green from where the W3 or 184 bus can be caught to the Palace or the Alexandra Park Road entrance to the park respectively.

This walk can be extended to Mill Hill (8.5).

6.2 **Palmers Green** circular via Wood Green and Bounds Green *6.3 miles*

A leisurely exploration of the 'green' remaining in Bounds Green, Palmers Green and Wood Green including Woodside Park and Broomfield Park.

It is our behaviour towards what we consider to be the shortcomings of others which is the real test of our worth. *Augustine*

Follow Walk 5.3 across Bounds Green Road through Woodside Park and then north to reach the Pymmes Brook on Chequers Way. Continue using the reverse of Walk 4.5 crossing the North Circular and walking through Palmers Green and Broomfield Park back to Alexandra Palace.

6.3 **Totteridge** via Finchley Lido returning by underground or bus *6.3 miles*

A walk to Totteridge via Coppetts Wood, Finchley and the Dollis Valley Green Walk

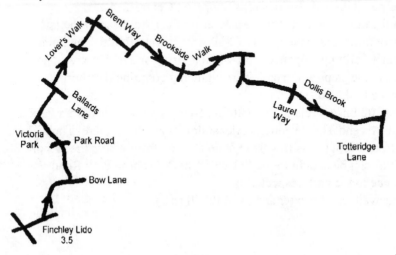

It is not what you are or have been that God looks at with his merciful eyes, but what you would be. *The Cloud of Unknowing*

Follow Walk 3.5 to Finchley Lido. The footpath exits at a small roundabout. Continue to the end of Leisure Way onto Finchley High Road. Cross the road, and continue left past Barnet Professional Development Centre and the shops, following the pavement round into Bow Lane. The Lane passes the perimeter of Fallow Corner playing field. Turn left well before Finchley Memorial Hospital into the footpath labelled for Queens Avenue. Continue straight ahead down Park Crescent.

At the junction with Etchingham Park Road cross over to enter the Victoria Recreation Ground. Turn left and continue to the path junction distinguished by the large tree. Turn right, heading down the park to the exit, with the children's playground on your left, to enter Long Lane, opposite St. Paul's Church. Turn right and continue to the junction with Ballards Lane and then turn left to cross at the pelican. Turn left and immediately right down the footpath between two shops.

Continue down the pathway, crossing Grove Avenue and passing over the railway (underground Northern Line) down to Nether Street. Turn right, then after fifty yards, left at the public footpath sign. Continue down Lovers Walk until the first junction. Turn right then into Brent Way and continue. After some distance, turn left down Fursby Avenue. Fifty yards down on the right, enter Brookside Walk.

Follow down to cross the Dollis Brook and continue in the same direction through Woodside Park, passing the play area on your left. Cross Lullington Garth maintaining the same direction along the signposted 'Dollis Valley Green Walk' until the path reaches Southover. Turn right along this road and continue past the Old Finchleians Memorial Ground to Tillingham Way. Turn right, following the sign for Dollis Valley Green Walk, and then left, as the road bends, onto the labelled footpath. Continue along the Riverside Walk, skirting the sports ground on the left. Cross Laurel Way and continue along the Dollis Brook right up to Totteridge Lane.

Catch the underground south to East Finchley and the 102 bus to The Avenue off Alexandra Park Road. Alternatively turn right and walk up Totteridge Lane to the High Road to catch the 234 bus to Arnos Grove, changing there to the 184 bus for Alexandra Park Road.

This walk can be extended to Chipping Barnet (8.1).

Seven Mile Walks

7.1 **Finsbury Park** circular via Haringey Passage and Parkland Walk *6.5 miles*

A circular walk that starts by crossing the streets of Haringey by the famous Passage and ends in the more rural atmosphere of the Parkland Walk

Unhappiness is the refusal to suffer. *George Scott-Moncrieff*

Follow Walk 3.6 via Haringey Passage. The route enters the Park from Endymion Road after crossing the railway bridge. Turn right at the entrance and continue along the road skirting the boating lake and cafeteria on your left. To return along the Parkland Walk turn right onto the pedestrian footbridge over the railway after the fenced hard courts. Continue along the old railway track to leave the Walk at Highgate, ascending Holmesdale Road to Archway Road. This route follows the reverse of Walk 4.1.

Turn right and walk up Archway Road crossing the top of both Shepherd's Hill and Muswell Hill Road. Opposite Church Road enter the Archway Gate of Highgate Wood.

Bear left past the toilets and children's playground to follow the track with the Sports Ground to your left. Turn off to the left passing to the right of Highgate Wood Information Centre and the Cafeteria. Turn right at the small car park. Keep straight ahead, heading towards the small Obelisk Drinking Fountain. Keep on in the same direction here, leaving the main tracks to ascend into the Wood behind the seat and bin just to the left of the Fountain. Continue straight ahead at the small clearing on the top of the incline and then descend towards the Cranley Gate.

Follow the directions back to Alexandra Palace from here as given at the end of Walk 3.4.

7.2 **Gordon Hill** via Broomfield Park, Grovelands Park and Enfield Town Park *6.7 miles*

The railway line followed on this walk was instrumental in the growth of the different suburbs. Sufficient green space and woodland remain on the route to provide refreshment and to evoke the age when charcoal-burning in the forest was the major industry.

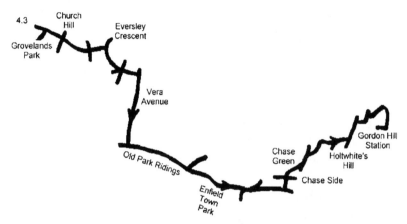

Obedience is not so much the forgoing of what we desire but the binding of all our energies to what God desires. *Lionel Thornton*

Follow Walk 4.3 to Grovelands Park but continue straight ahead at Grovelands Bowling Club to leave the park at Church Hill. St Paul's Church and the Quaker Meeting House are up the hill on the right.

Cross the road to enter Stone Hall Road. At the junction cross slightly to your left and enter the track beside 39 Houndsden Road. Continue to the end and turn right into Eversley Crescent. At the junction with Green Dragon Lane cross straight ahead into Maxim Road, turning right at the end into Vera Avenue. Continue down, passing St. Peter's Church and Grange Park railway station. Pass under the railway bridge and down to the end of The Grangeway.

Turn left up Old Park Ridings and walk up the hill. As the road flattens and bends to the left, turn right into Carrs Lane. After a short distance take the left-hand fenced footpath down through the golf course. At the end cross the old course of the New River and either turn left along the river bank or continue through Enfield Town Park towards Church Street, via Cecil Road if the walk visits the park and cafeteria. Cross Church Street towards Trinity Church and continue down to The Stag pub. Take the left hand footpath beside The Stag called Gentleman's Row. Note 'The Coach House' built as a barn in the sixteenth century, and the archway at the top of Chapel Street.

At the end of Gentleman's Row take the path over the stream and continue straight ahead through the cutting to Chase Side. Cross the road onto Chase Green and take the path diagonally to the right. At Green Avenue turn left under the railway bridge and then right to follow Monks Close and Monks Road down to Holtwhite's Hill. Take a left turn up the hill, turning right after a short distance into Hedge Hill. Continue around to the left and then take the right hand turn into Lee View. As the road rejoins Hedge Hill turn right and take the short pathway up on to Lavender Hill.

Turn right at the pavement and continue over the railway. Turn right again into Gordon Hill station to catch a train to Alexandra Palace station. As an alternative continue the walk to Trent Park and back to Alexandra Palace following the reverse of Walk 8.2

7.3   **Coppetts Wood** circular via Friern Barnet and Muswell Hill *7.3 miles*

The old hospital at Friern Barnet faces Alexandra Palace across the North Circular Road. This walk encircles the hospital site and visits the fascinating St. Pancras Cemetery, returning through the suburb of Muswell Hill.

In the hands of God mud is as transparent as light. *De Caussade*

Follow Walk 2.2 and continue past New Southgate station, turning left at the roundabout onto Friern Barnet Road. Continue past the old hospital and St. John's Church to the Town Hall. Turn left down Colney Hatch Lane, and after some distance cross the lane to enter Coppetts Wood. From the entrance continue, passing up the steps and taking the right turn at the junction to walk on to the exit gate.

On leaving the wood turn left to reach the North Circular Road and cross the pedestrian footbridge. Turn left along the Circular pavement to head east along the Cemetery fence. Turn right to enter

St. Pancras and Islington Cemetery, open until late afternoon. Cross the Cemetery to one of the western exits onto North Finchley High Road. Turn left and continue down the High Road. Take a left turn down Creighton Avenue and then right down Ringwood Avenue. Follow the directions at the end of Walk 4.6 and then Walk 3.4 to return from here via Highgate Wood and the Parkland Walk to Alexandra Palace.

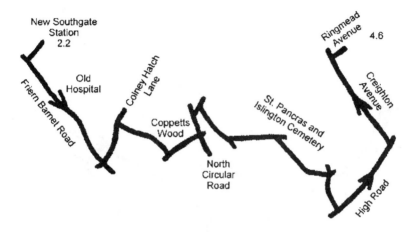

Alternatively from the end of Twyford Avenue turn left and then right following Fortis Green Road. At St. James, Muswell Hill continue straight ahead down St. James Lane. Join the Parkland Walk via the steps on the right at the old railway bridge, continuing via The Grove to Alexandra Palace as in Walk 3.4.

Eight to Twenty Mile Walks

8.1 **Chipping Barnet** via Finchley Lido and Totteridge returning by 184 Bus *8.3 miles*

Chipping Barnet, also known as High Barnet, was formerly in Hertfordshire and retains its ecclesiastical links with St. Alban's Abbey and Diocese. This walk via Finchley and the Dollis Brook exploits the 184 Bus route to the northern boundary of Middlesex.

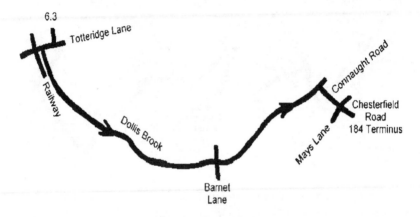

It is only by submitting to trial that an individual can learn to know what is in him. *Francis Chichester*

Follow Walk 6.3 to Totteridge Lane. Cross to the Post Office and turn right. Turn left to continue along the Dollis Valley Greenwalk. The Greenwalk follows the Dollis brook upstream from the River Brent to its source near Arkeley. This section of the walk runs parallel to the underground line built by Great Northern Railway in 1872. The footpath also runs parallel to a cycle track.

At Barnet Playing Fields, turn left, keeping to the brook. In the far distance, the tower of Barnet Church is prominent. St. John the Baptist Church, enlarged between 1871–5 by William Butterfield, remains a parish of St. Alban's Diocese. Chipping or High Barnet was formerly part of Hertfordshire. The ecclesiastical link with St. Alban's Abbey, which established a market here in 1199, remains, although Chipping Barnet is today part of north London.

Cross Barnet Lane at the traffic bollards and continue in the same direction, as the Greenwalk is joined by the London Loop and Red Circular walks.

After the housing estate on your right, ascend to view a splendid wooded horizon. The track enters Dollis Brook Walk at the bottom of Alan Drive. Continue straight ahead along the pavement, then follow it round to the right, ascending Connaught Road. At the top of Connaught Road, cross Mays Lane to the terminus of the 184 bus, at the bottom of Chesterfield Road. Travel back from here to the park entrance on Alexandra Park Road.

This walk may be extended into a circular walk returning to Alexandra Palace via Brent Cross using Walk 8.5.

8.2   **Trent Park** circular via Cockfosters and Gordon Hill   *15 miles*

This grand circuit of North London follows the Pymmes Brook upstream on its way north. From Trent Country Park the walk heads east to Chase Farm Hospital and Gordon Hill. The southern route traverses Enfield Town, Grovelands and Broomfield Parks, returning over the railway tunnel to Alexandra Palace.

To thine own self be true, thou canst not then be false to any man.
Polonius in Shakespeare's Hamlet

Follow Walk 5.6 to Cockfosters Road. Turn left and continue past the underground station to enter Trent Country Park at the Cockfosters Road Gate. The Park, now maintained by Enfield Borough, originated in the enclosure of part of Enfield Chase in 1777. The Sassoon family transformed the main house, now part of Middlesex University. During the Second World War the park was used as a prisoner of war camp.

From the Cockfosters Road Gate continue to the little Obelisk. Take the left fork there, walking to the right of the caféteria but to the left of the standing map onto the mud track. Follow London Loop signs until they lead away from the lake up into the woods. Continue along the lakeside path until it veers right down to the lake.

Before the red field gate turn left into the wood. Continue for a

hundred yards or so along the field
edge to a wooden fence. Turn right
to continue on the bridal path beside
the field. At the end of the field turn
left to head up the hill along the
eastern boundary of the wood. As the
track turns left cut into the bridal path
and turn right to reach the stile onto
Hadley Road.

Cross the road and turn right,
walking along the footpath, passing
Parkside Farm and the Pumping
Station. At the junction of Hadley
Road and the Ridgeway turn right, to
pass Chase Farm Hospital. Turn left at
the roundabout into Lavender Hill.
Continue to Gordon Hill railway
station. The circular walk returns to
Alexandra Palace by the reverse of
Walk 7.2.

8.3 **Hadley Wood** circular via Cockfosters and Chipping Barnet *17.5 miles*

*This circular walk moves out through
urban streets to join the Pymmes
Brook Trail in Arnos Park. From
Cockfosters, the route travels west
through the open countryside of
Hadley Wood and then south along
the Dollis Valley Greenwalk. The last
stretch runs east parallel to the North
Circular Road through Coppetts
Wood and back to Alexandra Palace.*

Without faith we will never understand the
source of our own love and goodness and

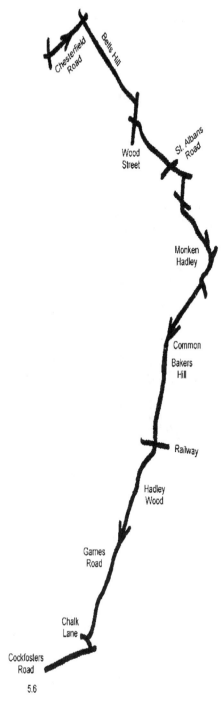

without doubt we will infect them with our prejudice and partiality.
Lionel Blue

Follow Walk 5.6. Turn left from Cockfosters Road along Chalk Lane passing Christ Church. Turn left towards the end of the Lane along Games Road continuing on the footpath through Hadley Wood. Cross the railway line onto Common Bakers Hill and Hadley Road to arrive in Monken Hadley.

'Monken' refers to the original hermitage linked in the twelfth century to Walden Abbey in Essex. St. Mary's Church has its date of 1494 in arabic numerals on the west tower. There is a rare and distinctive copper beacon on the turret.

Continue from the Church past Livingstone Cottage towards the Great North Road crossing into Christchurch Passage to reach Christ Church, Barnet. Cross St. Alban's Road into Stapylton Road. Continue along the road passing the Methodist Church. At the roundabout cross Wood Street and take the left turning down Bells Hill. Turn left down Chesterfield Road to the 184 bus terminus.

Return from Chipping Barnet to Alexandra Palace down Connaught Road and along the Dollis Brook, following the reverse of Walk 8.1.

8.4   **Lee Valley Walk** via Stoke Newington and Edmonton Green   *17.7 miles*

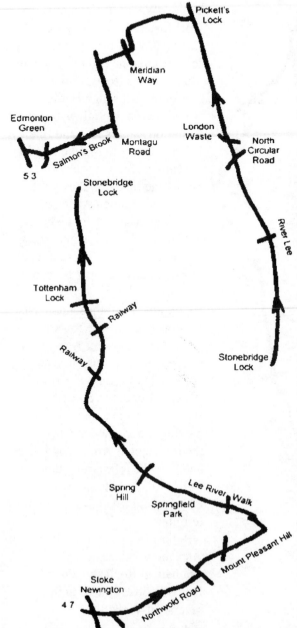

A circuit of Tottenham, travelling south-east through Finsbury Park and Stoke Newington to the River Lee and then north along the Lee Valley Walk to Pickett's Lock. The walk returns to Alexandra Palace along the Pymmes Brook and then south from Palmers Green.

The real voyage of discovery consists not in seeking new landscapes but in having new eyes.
Marcel Proust

Follow Walk 4.7 to Stoke Newington. On exiting from Abney Park Cemetery cross into Northwold Road. Pass West Hackney Almshouses on the left and Stoke

Newington Common on the right. Continue past Clapton Public Library. Cross the pelican at the junction with Upper Clapton Road. Turn left, then right into Mount Pleasant Lane continuing down Mount Pleasant Hill into Riverside Close. Take a right hand turn between blocks 119–130 and 131–142 to the River Lee (sometimes spelled Lea).

The Lee Valley Park extends 23 miles from the Thames at Poplar to Ware near Hertford. There is a 50 mile Lee Valley Walk that extends beyond the park to the source of the Lee at Luton. Improvements to navigation on the Lee can be traced from the twelfth century when the Abbot of Waltham Abbey instigated works. In the late eighteenth century the installation of a number of locks made the Lee a vital artery for London's trade. The twentieth century saw the construction of adjacent reservoirs like the King George's Reservoir (1913).

Turn left to follow the river walk under a railway bridge, passing The Anchor and Hope and Robin Hood pubs. The track skirts Springfield Park. Lee Valley Marina is evident at the Spring Hill Bridge.

After two railway bridges, note The Narrow Boat pub before Tottenham Lock. The Water's Edge pub and restaurant is found further north at Stonebridge Lock.

The walk proceeds under the North Circular at Cooks Ferry adjacent to London Waste Ltd. At Pickett's Lock cross the river and follow the Pymmes Brook Trail sign to the right, along Picketts Lock Lane. The lane passes the entrance drive to Lee Valley Leisure Centre and then bears sharp left to traverse Meridian Way. At the junction with Montagu Road turn left.

A short distance after the Town Crier pub and just before a garage, cross to enter the public footpath along Salmon's Brook to Plevna Road on the Pymmes Brook Trail. Cross the road to Edmonton Leisure Centre.

Continue up St. George's Road to The Broadway and Edmonton Green. Return to Alexandra Palace through Pymmes Park, Cambridge Circus and Chitts Hill following the reverse of Walk 5.3.

8.5   **Mill Hill** circular via Chipping Barnet and Brent Cross *19.6 miles*

Totteridge Common provides some of the most beautiful open space in north London. This marathon circular walk travels west through Coppetts Wood and Finchley, then north to Totteridge along the Dollis Brook. The walk crosses the Common to Mill Hill and continues south to Hendon. From Brent Cross the circuit is completed along the Mutton Brook through Hampstead Garden Suburb and East Finchley to the Alexandra Palace.

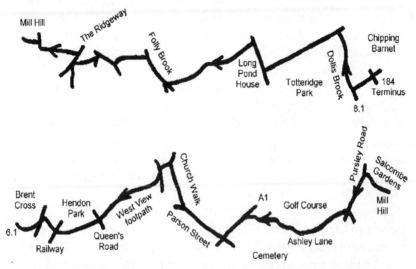

Memory is the force which can balance us, qualify and restrain the immediacy of modern desire strained way beyond itself by advertising and image. *John O'Donohue*

Follow Walk 8.1 to Chipping Barnet. Instead of turning up Connaught Road to the bus terminus, continue along the Riverside Walk. At the first stile continue across the track through a cutting in the hedge opposite and through a large field. At the far corner of that field continue through the gap in the hedge into another field. Continue along the left-hand hedge to the bridge in the far corner. Turn left over the Dollis Brook, and continue straight ahead following the line of the telegraph poles.

This pleasing rural path crosses Totteridge Park onto Horseshoe Lane. Turn right at the main road, and after a short distance cross the

road by the Long Pond House and enter the footpath beside the metal
gates. Proceed down the footpath, enjoying the view of Mill Hill.
The fine views at Mill Hill always attracted the wealthy as
inhabitants, often in grand secluded houses. The creation of Mill Hill
Broadway station in 1868 signalled the more popular development of
the suburb towards its present form which still retains the feel of its
rural origins.

At the junction turn right along the Folly Brook. At Folly Farm,
continue left along the metalled track which passes the cricket pitch.
The rather sinister edifice of the Ministry of Defence towers above.
At the road junction turn right along Burtonhole Lane. Take a left
turn down Eleanor Crescent, and after a short distance, right into a
cutting down to The Ridgeway.

Turn right, then after a short distance left following the signpost
'Public Footpath To Rushden Gardens' alongside the Kingdom Hall
of Jehovah's Witnesses. At the bottom, turn right into Rushden
Gardens and immediately left down Salcombe Gardens to Mill East
Church at the bottom. Turn left along Pursley Road, and then after
some distance, right down Ashley Lane. The lane becomes a
Bridleway after its junction with Oakhampton Road. Continue
between Hendon Cemetery and the Golf Course. The Bridleway
leads into Woodtree Close which goes down to the A1.

Turn left and continue for two hundred yards to the traffic lights.
Cross the A1 to ascend Parson Street. After some distance turn right
into Downage. Take the immediate left hand cutting called 'Church
Walk' which leads eventually to Church End and the ancient church
of St. Mary's, Hendon, between The Greyhound and Chequers pubs.
St. Mary's Church has a remarkable interior well worth a visit The
Gothic revival architect Temple Moore's 1914–15 additions respect
and harmonise with the thirteenth and sixteenth century elements.

Turn left past The Chequers, down Church End, and left again into
Church Road, crossing at the zebra. Turn right before the Chemist's
and then immediately left down West View footpath. This pathway
traverses a number of roads en route to Hendon Park. After crossing
Queens Road into the park, cross diagonally to exit the park by the
railway bridge. Continue along the footpath under the bridge and
after the grass-covered roundabout cross the road. Enter the
pedestrian underpass labelled 'Brent Cross Shopping Centre'.

Return to Alexandra Palace via Hampstead Garden Suburb (6.1).

Further Reading

A History of Muswell Hill Ken Gay Hornsey Historical Society 1999

Country Walks around London Geoff Garvey and Leigh Hatts Mainstream 1998

Down at the Old Bull and Bush Clive Smith Allied Domecq Leisure

Lee Valley Park Ordnance Survey 1996

Palace on the Hill Ken Gay Hornsey Historical Society 1994

Pymmes Brook Trail Leaflets Countryside Management Service

The Buildings of England: London 4: North Bridget Cherry and Nikolaus Pevsner Penguin 1998

The London Encyclopaedia Ben Weinreb and Christopher Hibbert (Editors) Papermac 1983

Walk the Loop : Section 17: Cockfosters to Enfield Lock Enfield Borough 1998